Sue +
Dore
26.6.16
Keep
SUFFERING
Always - a treasure.

In the Same Series

FRIENDSHIP

LOVE

Future Titles

FAITH

FAMILY

HOPE

SUFFERING

by
Georgette Butcher

in the series
Quiet Times

Collins

FOUNT PAPERBACKS

William Collins Sons & Co. Ltd
London • Glasgow • Sydney • Auckland •
Toronto • Johannesburg

First published in Great Britain in 1990 by Fount Paperbacks

Fount Paperbacks is an imprint of Collins Religious Division, part of the Collins Publishing Group,
8 Grafton Street, London W1X 3LA

Printed in England by Clays Ltd, St Ives plc

Suffering

28·5·16 Sat 7·30 AM ✓

I consider that what we suffer at this present time cannot be compared at all with the glory that is going to be revealed to us.

St Paul

28.5.16 Sat. 7.40 AM.

The word suffering covers everything that comes to us and causes either mental or physical pain. We may inflict ourselves with these, either by abusing our bodies or indulging in thoughts and actions which cause unhappy repercussions. Alternatively, it may come through other people, through natural causes, an earthquake for example, or we may suffer an illness for which there appears to be no reason. ✓

Paul tells us, in the second letter to the Corinthians, all that he suffered as an apostle of Christ — a formidable list of pain, imprisonments and catastrophes. He is yet able to say that the sufferings of the present time cannot be compared with the eternal glory that awaits us. ✓

Suffering, like so much else, has to be acknowledged and worked through. Many who have suffered, or do suffer, find that as they look to him, the Lord helps and teaches them. The pain is still there, it still has to be borne, but living each day with him means having his strength and support and a close relationship. Each day also leads on to the day when the glory will be revealed and there will be no more pain. ✓

13.5.16 28.5.16 7.40
Am - Sat

It is a great mystery that the suffering which God never intended is not only allowed by him but is even used for his glory. √√

Andrew Knowles

"I can do everything through God who gives me strength" Christ -

"All things work together for the good of those who love God & are called according to His purposes."

"The Lord is my strength & my song and He has become my Salvation"

13.5.16 28.5.16 7-40AM
Sat.

The knocks which we receive in life are the things which cause our characters to grow. Andrew Knowles suggests that if life were a primrose path we should have no need of God.

When the world was first made it seems that it was intended that we should have an unbroken communion with God. The entry of sin changed everything, including the turning away of mankind from God. The way back came through the sufferings of Jesus, but did not include taking suffering out of the world. So God uses it to reveal his glory.

The way in which we handle suffering in our lives can help others to know something about God. As we show that he is able to support us, we are proclaiming our trust in him. He uses the suffering to refine us, to lead us into greater dependence upon him, and always — as we go forward with him — we find that with the pain comes peace.

We must never think that our belief in God means immunity from suffering. It is only as we acknowledge it and bring it to God that it can be worked through and worked out.

13.5.16 Fri 4·15pm 28·5.16
Sat 8am

In my experience the wounds of poverty and suffering produce a special, very precious, very sweet honey.

Carlo Carretto

Carlo Carretto was a Little Brother of the Gospel. When he was in the novitiate he dreamt of living with the Alpine rescue teams up on the Matterhorn, and going with them to help people caught in storms. All his life he had been a mountain-climber.

One day, with the best of intentions, a friend injected him by mistake with a paralysing poison. In less than twenty-four hours his leg was useless, and the dream was over. Thirty years after, he was writing that he could not say that what had happened was not a misfortune, but that God was able to transform it into grace.

It is often from those who themselves have passed through deep waters that we can best accept help when the waters threaten to overwhelm us. When we see others with a similar disability, or who have had to suffer in the same way as ourselves, we can realize that in their acceptance of it in God, it is also possible for us to accept. It is not just acceptance, it is allowing Jesus to reveal himself as the one who has also suffered and is therefore able to succour us, and who has grace sufficient for us for every day of life.

13.5.16 28.5.16 8.10 AM
Satr

Such is the transforming of circumstances; not by their abolition but by the lifting of them into the orbit of a crucified and risen Jesus.

Michael Ramsey

28.5.16 Sat. 8.10 AM

It is possible to become immune to all suffering except our own. To be so concerned with our own little world that the greater world is forgotten. It is possible so to concentrate on the things that touch only us that we forget that we have our release and freedom at the expense of a life. It is possible to forget the cross.

It is not only that our sufferings need to be placed alongside the sufferings of Jesus and so brought into perspective, it is that we have power through his suffering. A power that can transform the details, situations, circumstances of life, and is something that we need to enter into. Amen

We forget that the cross is an entrance. It is the way to God, to forgiveness; but it is also the entrance to the riches that are ours as his children. Amen

Our circumstances can be transformed for us as we remember the cost to Jesus of our liberty. Meditating on what Calvary meant for him can change our thoughts about our problems. He is a risen Christ, and his resurrection means that he is alive. Alive to give his support and strength to all who need it. 13.5.16 4-30PM Fri

Jesus is ALIVE.

Friday, 3rd June 2016

It is given to some to teach, others to work and some to suffer as a ministry. See Something Beautiful for God.

F.B. Meyer

Louise Jordan Coastlands

11.47 PM. Coastlands has a healing service.

The opposite of illness is wholeness, and the bridge between the two is healing. Some think that healing should come automatically after the onset of illness, and if this does not happen, either for themselves or those around them, then there has to be a reason. It is usually made out that this comes from a lack of faith, sin, or a wrong attitude. Even today, in our churches and fellowships, there are Job's comforters who do not hesitate to put forward reasons why someone who is sick is not healed. Your will, not mine - be done

It does seem that prayer for direct physical healing is not always answered. We cannot demand that God does as we wish. As his children our asking must always be in the knowledge that he answers as is best for us within his plan for our good. We also have to learn how to ask, especially if the answer we want fails to come. It may mean that we should be praying in another way. I have plans to prosper you not to harm

Perhaps it is simply that our suffering, as F.B. Meyer suggests, is to be our ministry: allowing God to be seen in our lives in spite of the burden that has to be carried. Those who can do it become a blessing to others. you, the Lord says to Jeremiah the boy prophet. 1v9

3.6.16 12 midnight. 4.6.16
9.15PM

Rejoice in the Lord always.) again I say
Rejoice. Let your gentle
ness be evident to all - for
your Lord is near at hand"
Philli 4,13 I think!

St Paul

4.6.16 9.15 PM Sat. 366 times in the bible; do not

Because we are human and a prey to many fears, to suggest to any who are passing through difficult times that we should rejoice only brings a negative response. fear!

When bad times come upon us we can often only think of ourselves. Paul, however, reminds us that our lives are linked with God. William Barclay translates these words, "Never lose your Christian joy". We need to hold on to our relationship with God at all times.

Instead of going away from him, we need to concentrate more on prayer and reading his Word to remind ourselves of his love and care. We shall find that we are comforted and more able to believe that he will undertake for us.

Our joy comes from the assurance of belonging to him, that he is our Father and that he knows everything about us and has promised not to leave us. We need have no doubt of his love, for we need only remember the way of the cross that Jesus took for us. Our joy is that we belong to God. Things may not be good at this moment, but we are not abandoned, and as he has given us this life so we have the hope of life in eternity. Amen

5.6.16 Sunday.

There is the way of rebellion and bitterness, and the way of acceptance and submission.

Katie Wiebe

26.6.16 Sunday 4.40 AM

When things go wrong it is so easy to blame it all on God. He should have intervened — made things go differently. We make him the author of all the bad things that happen to us and even turn on him in rebellion. Instead of saying, "Why should it happen to me?" we should be saying, as the mother of a mentally retarded child did, "Why shouldn't it happen to me?" see Something beautiful

As long as we work through the anger and the rebellion, coming out the other side, not with resignation, but a true acceptance, then the situation can be used. for God.

It can be used to help us understand ourselves and how to face life itself. To stop shouting at God means having the time to listen to what he is trying to say to us in our distress. To cease showing rebellion by our attitude, to those around us, brings a reality into our love and a deepening of relationships.

Transforming bitterness into acceptance brings an inner peace that enables a calm tackling of the problem, and in submitting to the inevitability of the situation we emit a peace that helps those around us.

26 6.16 Sunday 4.45AM ✓

When life hits a Christian on the chin it tilts his face upward to look on the face of God. ✓

Selwyn Hughes

* but she and Carol are grieving over Papa John's cancer.

26.6.16 Sunday 4-45 AM

There are plenty of little things which happen daily that strengthen us in our Christian life as we outwork them, but it is when we stagger under a hard blow that we find ourselves turning to God.

Carlo Carretto, with a crippled leg, is able to say: "God loves his children and when he sees that someone or something has hurt them, what imagination he has — to transform the evil into good, inactivity into contemplation, the cry of pain into a prayer, grief into an act of loving."

Jennifer Rees Larcombe, in middle life struck down by illness and now in a wheelchair, writes: "Suffering seems to give Christians the opportunity to grow spiritually, more than anything else." Jen is now healed x

Margaret Spufford writes: "When the discomfort has become so great that I can do nothing but lie down, and cannot think clearly, then I know my work has become prayer. While I am still sitting at my desk, I am still a historian."

It seems that God becomes more real as our need becomes greater. There are few who would give up the pain if it meant losing God. We suffer most when we do not allow him in.

26 6·16 5am Sunday ✓

God uses suffering in pursuance of his purpose to make us holy. ✓

John Stott

26. 6. 16 5am Sunday

Holiness is something that we cannot discount. It is not an optional extra. God has said that we are to be holy; it is a fundamental requirement for entry into heaven. As we walk along the Christian path, God teaches us, so that we shall become holy — because he is holy. So much needs to be done in our lives, but it can hurt as we submit ourselves to his hands. He may have to allow things to happen to us: sickness, disappointments and failure, loneliness, are the ways in which we begin to understand not only ourselves, but God. The more we see our own weakness, the more we understand God's power and are convinced of our need of him. ✓

Although God allows to come into our lives those things which he then uses for our good, he is not oblivious to what the cost is to us. He is right alongside, going through the fire with us, giving strength to bear the pain. We may need to cry to him continually, yet he will still patiently bear with us. He is the Father who has to discipline his children in order to promote the holiness which he desires to see in us. ✓

27. 6. 16 Monday

All are weak because all are afraid.

Paul Tournier

We are weak if we allow ourselves to be submerged by fear. We may be afraid of something, but the very fact of recognizing the fear is a step forward out of weakness.

Grace Sheppard knows what it is to live with paralysing fear, made rather worse that as the wife of a Bishop she is a public figure. She says, "Facing fear squarely, and with professional help, I discovered how to manage it. It is", she writes, "all right to be afraid, but not all right to let it do the driving."

It is also all right to seek help, all right to lean on the love and support of family and friends, and at the same time to realize that God is somewhere in it all.

The words "Fear not" appear many times in the Bible, so we can see that God acknowledges our fear and knows the fears that beset us. If we just allow them to dominate life then everything becomes dull and useless. God is ready to help in this as in all else, but we have to make the effort and trust him to give the strength as we go forward. As Grace Sheppard says after one effort, "The fear evaporated; I felt fully alive".

God is not the *Author* of all events, but he is the *Master* of all events.

David Seamunds

Romans 8 v 28 reads: "And we know that in all things God works for the good of those who love him . . ." The trouble is that we so often fail to "know", or knowing we decide to disbelieve. Before we can take God's word and use it, we have to believe it. In moments of depression it is only too easy to dismiss even faith and trust, and wallow in aloneness. Somehow, we have to cause our will to take hold of his words — to remember times when he has not let us down, and to believe that even in "this" he is in control.

Our Christian walk is one of continually learning. We err when we think that as soon as we believe then everything will be known and so become easy. It is not like that. Most of us have to grapple with spiritual truths, learning and relearning as events come upon us. Having taken hold of one truth we then reach up to the next. God uses the things that come into our lives to help us climb. Some he may bring to show us how to climb, but always he is the master, concerned only for our good.

(God) uses every occasion to illumine us and his illumination is often perceived in darkness.

Ruth Burrows

We are surrounded by the evidence of the existence of God. Everything that is good and beautiful reminds us of him, yet we can be so involved with life as it appears to us that our world can seem to be an impenetrable darkness.

Worries about our families, jobs, health, the world situation, nuclear waste, the ozone layer, and much more, take up our energy and time. If life is looked upon only from this standpoint then a pall of gloom and uncertainty falls on us; but God can penetrate, and indeed seeks to do so, the darkness of our thoughts and the pessimism of our hearts. He uses these things to remind us that he is sovereign, that we must use our faith and trust to help us in understanding that he is in control. The world is upheld by its creator and we his creatures are his responsibility; he has undertaken to care for us.

It is when the darkness comes that we should seek his answers. Instead of turning away in despair it is the time to be guided by him and to allow him to teach us. The light that he gives enables us to go forward, and to find that next time darkness comes it does not seem so impenetrable.

God is not a judge and executioner, but a teacher.

David Watson

We have to accept that Christians are not exempt from the normal vicissitudes of life. This is possibly for two reasons: we are a part of the world in which we live, and it is an imperfect world; God wants to refine and teach us, and he teaches us through our circumstances.

Job was tested, for God allowed Satan to work in his life. Paul had a "thorn in the flesh" which God would not take away. We know that God does bring us to the test, just as we realize that it is the times when circumstances hurt us that God uses to teach us.

David Watson suggests that we should not ask "Why?" Our concentration should be on the fact that God knows — he is not indifferent — and all his help and strength is available to us. He wants us to use the time to learn.

It is no use acknowledging God as our teacher if we refuse to study the lessons. When we talk with him and try to be honest about our feelings, that is the time when he can help us to understand ourselves and know him more.

A desert is a sign of Christian maturity not of failure.

Jennifer Rees Larcombe

A spiritual desert is the place in which we find ourselves when, for one reason or another, we feel out of touch with God. It could be in illness or through disaster; problems for which there seem to be no answers; or just a realization one day that God no longer seems to be there for us.

Sometimes it is enough not to panic, and to go on quietly trying to hang on to a word of Scripture and the belief that as the sun sometimes hides behind a cloud but is still there, so does God appear to be hidden from our sight for a time.

The desert is always a place of temptation: doubt; fear; anxiety; anger; resentment; a whole range of emotions which can cause the darkness to be overwhelming. What in fact God is wanting us to do is to tackle these as they attack us, to see them for what they are. It is then that we gain strength.

We must, however, try to believe that God is there, walking along with us, for he has promised never to leave us; and the other side of the desert brings light and a new joy.

Everything he does is marked by love.

Mark R. Little

We have to admit that God does with us as he wills. He allows much into our lives that causes us distress. It is the way in which we react that is so important to the way in which we are able to cope.

In the letter to the Romans we read: "All things work together for good to those who love God." The "good" may be learning new lessons for this life or in preparation for the next, but the most important thing that we have to grasp and hold on to, is the knowledge of his love for each one of us.

In trusting his love we can acknowledge that his dealings with us must have a purpose. Love suffers with the beloved, feels the pain, enters the darkness. Love means caring, and God cares. Love means knowing and understanding, and God knows and understands our every reaction. Every blow that reaches us he knows about, and he is by our side even when we feel most alone.

Our comfort must be drawn from these things, and the realization that our love for him can deepen through our sufferings as our lives become more linked with his.

Every time I am forced by circumstances or my own stupidity to enter into darkness and suffering, I emerge battered but richer.

Sheila Cassidy

It is important that we realize the options that are ours when suffering comes into our lives. To withdraw or to become passive are possibilities, but Sheila Cassidy, writing of her experiences in a Chilean prison, tells of the struggle to abandon herself to God. She faced the question: if we give our lives to God, do we desire to take them back when the going gets difficult? Our raging against circumstances merely uses up our strength. We somehow have to accept what is happening to us in order to find freedom.

We also have to face the fact that God does not make everything easy for us. There *is* struggle, as Sheila Cassidy found when day after day she sought to let go and hand herself over to God. The struggle comes from our side as God seeks to draw us deeper into himself, and we fight against what we think is too high a price to pay.

Having gone through the experience, most seem to say that it has been a means of enrichment. It has been a means of finding out more about oneself but also of finding out more about God.

In a world like this it makes sense to stay close to the shelter.

Joni Eareckson Tada

The Psalms of David give a most vivid picture of the ups and downs, trials and tribulations that beset men and women in this life. David mirrors our thoughts as he tells of his despair and then goes on to reveal his trust in God. It reminds us that we are all very much alike in our thinking and reactions.

In Psalm 61 David says that he is faint; overwhelmed; and he needs "the rock that is higher than I". What we need in a world that sometimes tosses us here and there is a strong rock, an immovable rock that cannot be swept away. A rock that will shelter us from the storm. "He alone is my rock", says David.

There is no one else on whom we can truly depend. God is a strong rock, a refuge and a shelter. Staying close to him is our protection when the storms come.

As Christians we often face temptations and testings. Satan delights to see us confused; around us those of the world watch to see how we act. We need to stay close to shelter.

It takes heroic charity and humility to let others sustain us when we are absolutely incapable of sustaining ourselves.

Thomas Merton

One of the burdens of our suffering is that we become incapable of "sustaining ourselves". This can be because of physical weakness when we need others to minister to us, or it may be that life causes us to be temporarily incapable of coherent thought and action.

When those who care lift the burdens from us and take on the task of helping us to live, receiving can be an additional suffering until we learn to accept. Jennifer Rees Larcombe, an active person until confined to a wheelchair, found it difficult to be a receiver until she realized that Jesus himself was dependent on others nearly all of his life. He told her that receiving in grateful humility was a part of sharing in the fellowship of his suffering.

For some, receiving results in irritability. That causes tensions and unhappiness to others until it can be understood that dependence on people is a part of God's "allowing" in our lives, along with everything else. That his support and strength is available for this as well as all else, and that it is something that can be worked through with him.

There are no pain-free short cuts to growth.

Jennifer Rees Larcombe

How should we learn patience, faith, trust and so much more if life and its circumstances were simple and easy? The Christian life is a life of growth, from the moment of decision to follow Christ, we begin to learn. Just as the child has to be taught to fit into its place in life, so does the disciple.

As a child learns by behaviour, reactions, coping with those things that it comes up against, so does the Christian. A child will cry because it does not always understand why it is refused something, it can be hurt until it begins to trust and knows that it is loved. Life can bring us much that makes us hurt, but we can allow God to transform us through them.

We need to change the "Why me?" cry into "Help me to understand how I can learn from this". It is not going through the jealousy, anger, resentment stage, but straight to the one of trusting. Allowing God to change us, to help us to grow, because if we are putting up defences, reacting negatively, it is difficult for him to reach us. If we want to grow we have to accept the pain, but in accepting the pain we not only grow but are upheld by God.

Every burden carried by us is also shared by him.

Basil Hume OSB

God's overwhelming desire is that we shall be one with him. He longs for us as no human can do, he knows that our true satisfaction can only be found in him and he yearns that we might find it. So, day by day, as we try to find our way towards the inner heart of God, he knows the struggles and burdens that are ours.

Perhaps for you there has been rejection; the knowledge that for some other person you have been deemed inadequate, unwanted. Jesus himself was rejected — his friends left him. The people he came to save shouted, "Crucify him!" Still today many turn away from him, they want nothing to do with the God who loves them.

Whatever is our grief at this time, he knows all about it. More than that he feels it with us and he will help us to bear it. As we remember his rejection and why he had to bear it, we are reminded of his love for each of us. He will not let us go, he stays close to us in order to share the burdens and to help us find the way.

It is often through pain and pressure that God can produce something very beautiful in our lives.

J. John

People look on at the suffering that they see Christians bearing and wonder why God allows it. It is assumed that the very fact of being a Christian should bring immunity from the anxieties and pressures that beset others.

J. John has written about a Christian missionary, who on becoming blind towards the end of her life was asked why she should have to suffer after all the years of service that she had done for God and other people. Her reply was, "I suppose God wants to put the finishing touches to my character".

God does not allow these things to pass us by because he knows that we can grow through them, that bearing them our dependence upon him grows and our relationship with him deepens. He looks to see if we trust him even through the trials being borne.

There will have been other problems and his faithfulness proved, here is yet another, but his deep caring love seeks only that the best shall come out of our pain. So it is that as we allow ourselves to rest in him, the joy of knowing him surpasses all the suffering.

For as long as he was capable of suffering, he suffered and sorrowed for us.

Julian of Norwich

When suffering comes to us, in whatever form, we can turn our minds to the life of Christ and acknowledge that never did man suffer as did the Son of God.

His was the suffering of a good man giving his life up to death in order that salvation should be available to the people of the world. It was God himself caring enough to bear the pain and humiliation, so that his people might have reconciliation and hope.

"Where is God?" we cry, as our personal world crashes around us. "My God, my God, why have you forsaken me?" cried Jesus on the cross. We have to acknowledge that because of us, for that moment, Jesus was alone; but because of it we can never be abandoned.

For thirty years Jesus lived and worked as one of us. For the three years of his ministry he moved out amongst people who often jeered at him, misunderstood him, sought to trap and humiliate him. The culmination was betrayal, a mockery of a trial and death on a cross when most of his friends forsook him. It was a suffering deliberately borne for us.

Death is a transition from life to life.

Dr Carl Henry

Part of the suffering involved with our own death comes from our fears of diminishing strength, pain and the unknown. When we are young we feel able to step out boldly on the path of life, but then we see what life can do, and it begins to dawn on us that there is a time beyond which we shall not be going on this earth.

We have put so much of our own meaning into the word "death" that it has clouded all that it really means. It should mean entry into a new existence, not the end of existence.

Death for the Christian means going into a new life — a life of which this one is but a shadow. There are times now when we know the presence of God in such a real and glorious way. Surely, this must be a foretaste of the next life.

Apart from all the things that we can be glad about because they will be no more, the things that we feel that we should miss will be forgotten once we walk in this new life. All will be better than we can possibly think or believe. We need to look at the things that man has not made to begin to understand.

If our hearts need to be broken, and he chooses this as the way in which they should break, so be it!

C.S. Lewis

Perhaps the hardest part of all our pain and suffering is the realization that this is the way that has been chosen for us.

God, who loves us, has chosen just this set of circumstances for us to live through, and until we can fit ourselves into them in a reasonably comfortable way, the actual suffering will be magnified, because we shall be at odds with the only one who is able to help us.

Commitment to God includes trusting him. Where is love and commitment when we harden our hearts against him? If our lives belong to him, should we be concerned with trying to fight our way out of what life is at the moment?

If we can acknowledge his lordship over us then we can also accept what he sends into our lives. If, in the midst of the pain that our problems and circumstances are causing us, we can trustingly look to him, we shall find that we have a companion who can help us to bear it all.

To be able to say, "So be it" is a part of the need to have a broken heart and a part of the lessons to be learnt.

If we really followed the Spirit we would be willing to go through suffering and crucifixion if need be . . . in order to bring life to others.

David Watson

There are divisions and rifts within groups of church people that cause pain and suffering to individuals. Difficulties arise that cause wounds that seemingly cannot be healed. Often it is easier to part company than to go on in situations that cause us distress. Walking away from a situation may not always be the right thing. Sometimes we take more note of our discomfort than in seeking to know the Lord's will and following it, especially if it leaves us with the suffering.

God does sometimes expect us to stay with a situation which we find distasteful, and who can know if that does not mean life to someone nearby? Praying and working at it within the circumstances may just be the right thing both for us and for others. It is too easy to give up when the going is tough.

The way to the cross was hard for Jesus. He too would have wished to step aside! "Save me from going through this bitter ordeal. But not what I will but what you will." His heart and will were set to do what his Father wanted, and it was the price of reconciliation.

There is rejoicing in the presence of the angels of God over one sinner who repents.

Jesus, Luke 15

If we ever think that we have gone too far away from God ever to be wanted by him, we must read the story of The Prodigal Son and believe that God is waiting to welcome us into his arms.

To feel that we are alone and an outcast can cause our lives to seem drear and without worth, but it is possible for the sun to shine, for life to become meaningful even though we may have gone our own way and done those things which we scarcely dare to dwell upon.

God loves us, and there is nothing that can separate us from him if we want to meet with him. There is a lovely thought written, that if we walk away from God and then turn back seeking him there will not be far to go. He will only be a step behind because he will have been following all the time.

We only have to say that we are sorry — sorry for the wrong things, sorry for disappointing him, and setting out on a new life with him will take away the inadequacies of a life lived apart from him.

There is no way to fruitfulness except through careful and relentless pruning.

Selwyn Hughes

It is in John's gospel that we read of God as a gardener. Jesus speaks of himself as the vine and his disciples — us — as branches. The object of the vine is to bear fruit, good fruit, and for this the branches have to be treated and pruned.

Jesus speaks of the gardener cutting and pruning, for in this way there will be fruit, better fruit than if there had been no pruning. We often hear how a gardener has cut a bush right back and the following season there has been an abundance of flowers or fruit. This is how God works in our lives.

Our Father is the gardener who knows exactly how to cut away that which is of no value or will hinder growth in our lives. We may not relish what is happening but it is the pruning which produces fruitfulness.

The gardener is always careful with his trees and shrubs. Our Father does his work well, gently and in love, glorying in a happy result. On our part we need to accept that it is only through the care and pruning that we shall produce fruit that is pleasing to him.

The value of suffering does not lie in the pain of it . . . but in what the sufferer makes of it.

Mary Craig

Two of Mary Craig's sons were born with severe abnormalities. We can imagine the feelings of a young mother, who having given birth to one problem child, finds later that she has a second. How does one begin to cope?

It is surely perfectly natural that when seeming disaster strikes, after the certainty has been acknowledged, that horror, dismay, and rebellion take over. We may even feel guilty, but there will certainly be many questions.

God does understand about the pain — and the questions — and he will show us what to do. "Bring all your worries to him to carry for you . . ." is William Barclay's translation of 1 Peter 5 v 7. Somehow we have to learn to keep lifting the problems from our shoulders to his, trusting him for the first thing, then the next as each comes up, using the suffering to draw on what God promises to do for us.

Would we seek his peace unless we were troubled? Or his grace unless we were distressed? The more we need, the more we are driven to him and the more we learn of his love and faithfulness. It is as we take the suffering and reach God through it, that we can find some sort of sense in it all.

It is very difficult to forgive from the heart, but as long as we withhold forgiveness we are refusing to let God be God in us.

Gerard W. Hughes

Many have deep hurts that refuse to heal as long as there is a refusal to forgive the person who has inflicted the wounds. We may not realize that this is the reason why life seems so bleak, why love is a stranger, and the heart within seems as cold and hard as a stone. If we cannot forgive it is not the one who inflicts the wound who suffers, so much as the one who will not forgive.

The New Testament is not silent on the question of forgiveness; each time that we say the Lord's prayer we are reminded that as we expect to receive forgiveness, so must we forgive. Because refusal means going against his will, it means that we cannot receive God in the way in which he wants to be in us.

If Jesus could say, "Father, forgive them . . ." about those who nailed him to the cross, is it not possible for us, who often fail, to forgive those who harm us? To be able to forgive brings not only healing but a restoration into our lives.

It's all right as long as you don't look down.

Robert Foxcroft

Robert Foxcroft was a church minister who contracted cancer and died in his mid-forties. As a radio broadcaster he was able to speak about his battle with the disease, and one of his analogies was to compare the illness with rock climbing.

If you are in the process of going up there isn't much you can do except to go steadily onward. The way may be difficult; progress incredibly slow; the body weary beyond thinking, and yet each toe hold has to be found and each hand hold tested. There is no point in looking downwards and adding to the problems, concentration has to be centred on just going forward.

It is not difficult to think of illness as a climb where the whole being is thinking of just going forward and time is measured by moments. There is a tremendous effort involved in just trying to cope. For each of us, one day, however brave the fight, there comes an end to it. Our journey has been to God, although he has also been with us on the way.

Death is freedom from the body's pain and its restrictions. Our inner being is released to find entry into its true home.

In solitude we can pay attention to our inner self.

Henri Nouwen

If we are afraid to be with ourselves then we need to learn how to be alone. To grow in the spiritual sense, we need to get to know ourselves, and we can only do this as we take the time to face up to what we are.

Not only do we need to learn to live with ourselves, but we also have to allow the growth of the inner self which comes from communication with God. To find God, we need to be alone with him, to allow the spirit to find and rest in him. In the quietness we hear the "still small voice". In the stillness our hearts meet his.

In the hurly burly of Christian fellowship we sing and praise together. We give and receive of each other, and we unite in our worship. In our quiet place we allow the healing power of Christ to deal with our wounds, to teach us how to go about living, to love our fellows, to forgive.

He allows us to draw close; when we refuse we are diminished and he mourns for us. As we try to cope with ourselves, by ourselves, we suffer.

The person who carries a secret has chained himself to a dungeon.

Gordon MacDonald

There are people walking our streets who know something about themselves — and it is as if they are carrying a heavy burden, or being chained to a dungeon.

It is not anything new — we read in the Bible that David, "at the time that kings go off to war", stayed at home and was led into adultery and murder. We are not actually told about David's feelings, but it was a secret that he had to carry day after day.

It can, and does, happen to many people. Whatever is the secret that has to be carried it can cause deep misery and suffering. The mixture of dread, remorse and fear, can be almost unbearable. The only way out from under all of this is to right the wrong.

We may mistakenly think that bringing everything into the open will mean worse pain, but all who have been able to bring themselves to do so refute that suggestion.

It was God who made David confront his secret and understand exactly what he had done. David was punished, but he found freedom from the guilt and burden of wrong-doing.

The fact of suffering undoubtedly constitutes the single greatest challenge to the Christian faith.

John Stott

It would seem that no one has found the true answer to the mystery of suffering. For it is a mystery, not so much that there is such a thing as suffering but that God does not intervene to take it away or to stop catastrophes happening.

We sometimes bring suffering upon ourselves by our own actions, or it can come by the actions of others, but what we also have to face is that suffering is a part of the world in which we live. It has been suggested that it matters less that we attempt to solve the problem of suffering than that we should find a means of coping with it.

Many who do not have a faith in God have yet managed to find a courage which has enabled them to cope with tragedy in their lives. For Christians, often the first barrier to be overcome is that of why a loving Father should allow terrible things to happen to his children. Perhaps it can only be overcome by letting God more fully into our lives and giving him our complete trust. It brings a totally different dimension when God is in the suffering with us.

His thoughts said, as I journey sometimes the water is bitter.

Amy Carmichael

Amy Carmichael's writings, not known so much now, have been a help to many on the Christian path. She knew the heart of the pilgrim and the stumblings and fears of the way, as well as being sensitive to what God was trying to teach.

Here she reminds us that if the Spirit is leading on the journey then the way may lead to Marah. We read in Exodus 15 that at Marah the Israelites could not drink the water because it was bitter, and Moses was told by God to throw in a piece of wood. Amy Carmichael writes of a Tree which "cast into the waters shall make the bitter waters sweet. One thought of Calvary will make any water sweet."

We have happy times and then there are others when "the water is bitter" and we become despondent. That is when we have need to remind ourselves of God's love, his personal love for each of us. A love which may first have become real to us as we realized the meaning of the Cross of Calvary.

Meditating on the suffering and love borne on that wooden cross by Jesus, the forgiveness and inheritance that is ours because of his death, then his grace and his peace will enter into us afresh and the journey will not seem so difficult.

A rock in this terrible sea.

Margaret Spufford

Margaret Spufford suffers from osteoporosis, which unusually made itself apparent at an early age. Her second child was diagnosed as having cystinosis, a rare metabolic disease, before she was one year old. Through all that her child had to bear, and all her own anguish, she felt that the only way she could support her daughter was by "trying to remain a rock".

To look on the suffering of others, and especially of one very close, is another kind of suffering, one that is heart-rending and worse than having to bear the pain oneself.

At the same time, as a Christian, the questions must still crowd in. The evilness of suffering has to be faced and Margaret Spufford writes, "I do not regard the evils which torment me as punishment from the hand of God, or signs of his wrath. I do, though, share [the] belief that these evils may be turned to his purposes."

Instead of having faith and trust in God for oneself there has to be the belief that it is well for the loved one. The belief that God does have a purpose through all that is happening, and that the spiritual progress of another is as important for them as it is for us. Help is given by strong support.

He spread his wings . . .

Deuteronomy 32 v 11

The story of the way in which an eagle learns to fly illustrates most vividly the way in which our Father/Mother God both loves us and is fearless in teaching us those lessons that are necessary for our growth.

Eagles take great care in building the nest, high up in a tree or mountain crag. It is well made with twigs, leaves and anything that can be found, and then it is lined with soft feathers. When the eggs are hatched the eaglets are well cared for, until one day everything changes. The eagle "stirs up the nest", no more soft lining, just hard and prickly twigs. The eaglet may well wonder what is happening as it teeters on the edge of the nest and then finds itself hurtling down. Its whole world has changed and there is only this terrifying drop. It is then that the eagle swoops and catches the eaglet on her wings. The pattern continues until the eaglet can fly.

God wants us to be strong in our faith and to enter fully into a vital life with him. Until it can fly the nest is the eaglet's only world; when it flies and soars up high its life is a whole new adventure.

An immense loneliness which nobody can penetrate.

Henri Nouwen

Jean Vanier founded L'Arche, a Christian community in which handicapped people and helpers live together. Henri Nouwen is priest-in-residence at one such community in Toronto. Of the deeply handicapped he says that they are sometimes in anguish and deep anxiety.

Agony of soul is a depth of suffering that can find no help except from the One who also suffered such agony. The Garden of Gethsemane witnessed the deep agony that Jesus went through as he contemplated the way he had to tread, and then upon the cross the darkness of complete aloneness was his.

The cross is the only answer to all our questionings. Here, we see God in Jesus, revealing through the shame of such a death his love for each of us. He bore more than pain and derision, he bore the weight of sin which caused the cry that the cup might be taken from him; yet he was committed to his Father's will.

This same Jesus is the one who understands our anguish; who knows about our frustrations; who does not condemn us. He is with us in all our grief and sorrow, and he is the one who will help.

The purpose of the dark night.

Thomas Merton

It is no use assuming that we can reach perfection in anything without much practice or without trial and error. Usually this means some despair and anguish before we even approach the ability we are seeking.

When we start out on the path of holiness it takes a whole lifetime even to begin to understand about the way we are taking. Along it we encounter much that causes dismay and doubt. We think that all must be simple, and then find that there is darkness where we expected light, fear when we expected to be confident. We feel that we fail not only God but ourselves, as we stumble along wondering if he cares.

We must first understand that all that enters our life can be a means of knowing God's grace. Everything that causes us to react can be a means of refining, but we do have to work our way through, with his help. The fear has to be turned into trust, we have to learn to abandon ourselves to him with a perfect love. As he leads us on it is always God's purpose to bring us through into maturity. The darkness may not be what we want, but the purpose is there.

Only a God whose love shares all pain from within can still our doubts and questions.

Cicely Saunders

Very often the reason why it appears that God is not answering our questions or helping us in our need is because we are not giving him the time to speak or to minister to us.

When we are so hurt that our minds are full of conflicting thoughts, and our hearts of bitterness and perhaps rage, it is almost impossible for God to reach us. If our anger is directed towards him, how can we expect to hear his voice through the noise of our self-pity?

So it is that we deny ourselves of the one who can bring peace into the disorder of our thinking. Our longing for love and support is not met until we actually turn to him. Once we recognize that he is the only one who can meet our need, and give him the time to do it, then we shall see that he can do for us all for which our hearts are crying out.

A God who has known pain and the pathway of suffering is the only one who can truly understand all that causes us anxiety. A God who loves us is the only one who can minister to our need.

The greatest lessons are potentially learned in deserts if one, in the midst of struggle, listens for God's call.

Gordon MacDonald

It is possible to be so taken up with the "struggle" that thoughts of anything else fail to enter our minds. Yet a desert is much more the place where we are likely to hear God speaking to us, than in the business of the city.

Jesus was led into the desert at the beginning of his ministry, where presumably he communed with his Father. Then he was tested. The Israelites, forty years in the wilderness, were led by God "to humble you and to test you", said Moses. John the Baptist was in the desert when he began baptizing. Was this, for him, a place of moulding, of learning, from God?

Deserts are barren, lonely places, to be avoided if possible, but if God leads there it must be for a reason. He may be wanting to remove the noise and bustle of everyday living, noise that shuts out the sound of his voice, in order that we really listen for him. When nothing is left for us and we turn at last to God then, in having our full attention, he can begin to teach. It is when we are stripped of the things that we consider important that we allow God to show that he is sufficient for us.

With many of us, much of our life is overgrown with useless things.

Selwyn Hughes

In his book *The Divine Gardener*, Selwyn Hughes tells of a friend who said, "Whenever I permit my spiritual affections to wander, God knows how to bring me to heel; He dries up the flow of my finances."

We have confidence in the abundance of our "goods", and in them we feel that we have safety. It is only when they are stripped away that we become aware that our life with God is of primary importance.

Much that happens to us may be our own fault, but there are many times when God intervenes in our circumstances to remind us of himself, simply because we are trusting in our own ability to provide for the family, hold on to power, be in a good job. Failure brings disillusionment and a sense of failure, and our ego is flattened; yet all the time God wants us to depend on him.

So he gently strips us of some of the things in our lives, in order that we may find him afresh and learn of his love and grace. Learn that he wants to be in the centre of our life, not pushed out on to the circumference whilst we occupy ourselves with the things that we consider important.

God seldom gives his people so sweet a foretaste of their future as in their deep afflictions.

Richard Baxter

It seems that when troubles surround us and the daily path is harder to tread, then we do receive from God some of his most precious moments.

If recognizing our need, we draw nearer to him and allow him to minister to us, we find that in the midst of the darkness, we have a strength that sweetens the pain.

Unfortunately, so often, we concentrate entirely on the thing which is causing us distress, and this shuts God out. It is when we share it with him that he can comfort and sustain us. It is not only that we receive from God the strength to go on day after day, but that there is a teaching and a learning process as we take time to be with him.

Because our need is great we turn to him more often and that allows the relationship to grow. It is in these times of our dependence and meeting with him that we have a glimpse of what will one day be a completion — a wholeness — which will be ours when we move from this life to the next.

It is as we go *through* the little deaths that resurrection follows.

Sylvia M. Lake

Dr Frank Lake did a great work through the founding of the Clinical Theology Association, but he was apparently not an easy man to be with. His wife admitted that there was a cost to the family for all that her husband accomplished, and yet she was able to see that in God's plan it became a means of grace.

Men and women can be driven by a purpose which takes away much of what passes for normal life. It can mean a suffering to those closest with which it is difficult for them to become reconciled. Only when it is brought to God and he is allowed to take the agony, disappointment, and loneliness is it transformed, becoming something worthwhile in the whole set-up of the circumstances.

Leaning on him brings a new trust; hurt feelings find healing because of his care; the knowledge of his love becomes a refuge. Sylvia Lake called them "little deaths", but resurrection makes death worthwhile. It is after death that new life comes, and then death is in the past. That is why we can say that it was worth going through *that* to get to *this*.

In reality all men are solitary. Only most of them are so averse to being alone, or to feeling alone, that they do everything they can to forget their solitude.

Thomas Merton

However close we may feel to another person there is still the fact that we are one alone. It becomes pain and suffering when we have not learnt that the solitary place we each have within ourselves is there to be filled by God with his presence.

So many people feel that as long as there is noise and movement, the continual activity will blunt the feeling of aloneness. But there must always come a time when darkness falls, all becomes still and we are left alone with our thoughts.

What we are can then dominate our thinking, whether we feel hard done by, resentful, fearful, even aggressive. It is at these times that if we can be honest with ourselves we can learn why we feel as we do and even turn towards God to allow him to deal with us. He is able to make us see why we are afraid of ourselves and our situation. He can make the solitary place change from a place of suffering into that of an at-one-ness with himself. We do not have to be alone, we can learn to live with God in such a way that we are always aware of his presence with us.

God matche(s) the challenge . . . with a special supply of his unfailing grace.

Selwyn Hughes

As a young girl, Corrie ten Boom came face to face with the fact of death when a neighbour's baby died. Distraught, she feared the eventual death of her father. "Corrie," he said to her, "when you and I go to Amsterdam — when do I give you the ticket?" "Why, just before we get on the train." "Exactly, and our wise father in heaven knows when we are going to need things too. Don't run out ahead of him, Corrie. When the time comes that some of us will have to die you will look into your heart and find the strength you need — just in time."

Each of us has to face bereavement, for death is a part of life, but in this and in so much of any sadness that comes to us, God is ready to give us what we need to cope. He does not give us his grace to store up for the time when our need is greatest, but neither do we have to fear that his grace will not be sufficient when we most need his strength. His promise will be fulfilled at the moment of our need.

Souls soon realize that a little bitterness is preferable to a surfeit of sweetness.

St Thérèse of Lisieux

We sometimes need to be taken to task for actions or attitudes, but how difficult we find it is to be reprimanded, even though we may realize that it is justified. Our natural self rises up in indignation, pride is hurt and the first thing we do is to show anger against the other person.

St Thérèse in her writings seeks to counsel, and mentions her dealings with others. She tells that a child during a painful operation is sure to cry out, but this would change to delight when able to run about and play.

The hurt that may be ours when we are attacked, our feelings bruised and we feel that those who should be helping us are instead pulling us down, can in the end be used to enable us to become a better person. A child given all it desires and allowed to do as it pleases is precocious and uninteresting, and eventually suffers because it has not learnt discipline. The lessons we have to learn in life are a means of blessing as God uses them to enable us to be more spiritual, more like himself.

The very things we dread can be those which form a richer pattern on our lives.

Hugh O. Douglas

Grace Sheppard writes about fears that can come into our lives and says, "Courage is waiting for us to take hold of it". There are many things that we have to do for ourselves. God is always there responding to our trust, but that visit to the doctor, the acknowledgement of a mistake, the entering into a new situation, can only be accomplished by actually doing it. Once done, the relief and glorious realization that we have been able to do it adds much to our self-worth.

It does not necessarily have to be something that anyone knows about. If we manage to do that from which naturally we would shrink, we have become a stronger person.

Sometimes it needs courage to tell others that we have some great fear, but it may be necessary to receive the kind of help that we are needing. Whatever we have to go through we shall be the stronger for having faced it.

Jesus tells us to have courage because in this world we shall have trouble. He also says, "I have overcome the world". His strength is therefore available to help us to take those steps which need to be taken.

I have learned to be content in whatever circumstances I am.

St Paul

Joni Eareckson Tada was in her teens when she had a swimming accident which left her quadriplegic. She would be the first to say that life is not easy, but she also says that God's Word has been, and is, a life line when she has felt herself drowning in despair. A promise to cling to when the waters are swirling around us, or more practically, when the long dark night has to be gone through.

Circumstances make up the life of each one of us. For some it is coping with life in a wheelchair, for another it is an unhappy marriage, and for yet others it is having to struggle on alone. Within the circumstances though, there is always God, and it is because of the circumstances and within them that the relationship with him can develop.

It is at once the hardest and yet the most wonderful thing to realize that it is just this situation that can cause us to respond to God, and that because of it we can be content even in all that surrounds us. To know the upholding and the friendship of God can be enough to get us through each day.

There are seeds within pain; seeds which eventually grow and yield a harvest.

Jane Grayshon

These words are written by a young woman who is in constant pain and who has had innumerable operations. When looking at her, she appears to be what she is, the wife of a vicar with two children to look after. She has found, as have so many others in her plight, that there is an end product, something that comes from the experience of the pain and the circumstances that accompany it. Instead of wasting time searching for reasons, there is a searching out for what can be reaped.

The very experiencing of pain can lead us into new paths of knowing God, for it means that in our need we may look to him to supply the help that we so desperately want. In the ravishes of sickness, the darkness of pain, we find new facets of God's giving. In the reaching out, in the clinging to God, in seeking to understand what he is saying through all these things, the seeds are beginning to grow.

The harvest is what can be reaped of beauty and growth, in partnership with God, from what some would see as barren ground.

Our Creator God who . . . does not blame us for not getting it right first time.

Grace Sheppard

A Christian sometimes feels such a failure, so despondent at the type of person he or she thinks that they are. It can even become disgust, and overflow into derogatory words as they look at themselves in the mirror, or stamp around the room.

We forget that God made us, and that his love endures; that Satan delights when we give in to the temptation of thinking that we are of little worth. Even if our parents reject us, God will receive us, we are told in Scripture.

We have to learn about the nature of God; to believe that if he has led us into the truths of redemption then he has a purpose for us. That once we are in the family of God we have total security; that he will treat us as a father, but as a perfect father.

We may feel afraid, unable to do what others seem to do, believing that we are not learning anything. God is not impatient, he will not mock us, nor, as he sees our desires, does he blame us if we get things wrong. Belonging to him does not mean that we are immediately perfect; it is the beginning of a process of sanctification.

Suffering can make us truly wise.

Ralph Martin

The trouble with writing about suffering is that it is easy to say things that to anyone suffering appear to be trite and mere platitudes. It is only as we suffer ourselves that we can work through our thoughts, and find whether there is any truth that means that out of suffering comes something good.

The suffering itself can be so black and impenetrable that it seems impossible to suggest that in the darkness there is hope and strength to be found; but through suffering we *can* find our greater need of God. If we can understand that he is using the suffering to make us grow as Christians, then our dependence on him, our trust and confidence in him, will also grow and we find that every hardship does lead us forward.

We also have something to give to others. What we learn of God's love; of patience; of understanding; can be passed on through deeds and words. The more we take from him, the more we have to give out to help other people. If we become wise through suffering then it is a wisdom that others may share.

The Lord is with me; I will not be afraid.

Psalm 118 v 6

Whatever age we attain, we are still as little children inside, often perplexed, troubled and afraid. We find ourselves in circumstances which it seems that we are helpless to do anything about. It is then, exactly like the tiny child we feel ourselves to be, that we look for a hand and the security of holding fast.

Our heavenly Father ministers to us as we open ourselves up to him. He listens and understands as we try to let him know just how we feel. Perhaps he needs to remind us that belonging to him means that we must trust him, both for ourselves and for those whom we love. As we think about trusting him we shall remember that he loves us and all the time is wanting us to get to know him more.

There is nothing which he will not bear with us, no time that he will leave us alone. Because he is with us, we can give him our fear and trust him to carry us through. It is when we refuse to acknowledge his presence that everything overwhelms us and seems so unbearable. We are not to expect everything to be made easy for us, life is not like that, but God always gives his help.

To be a Christian is to have your heart broken by the things that break the heart of God.

Tony Campolo

Our world is full of tragedies — people who are starving; children who are alone; sickness; homelessness; those who are exploited . . .

We put the blame on God when so often it is man himself that causes the pain by his indifference to the pain of others; by refusing to act where there is injustice; by wars; by selfishness. God looks at the world he made and sees the sadness of his creatures abandoned in their misery, and in his love he suffers with them.

As his children, Christians need to see the world through the eyes of God, and suffer with him as he enters the suffering of his people. As we come to know him so we also come to know his mind. We become sensitive to the way in which he looks upon things, and we begin to understand something of the pain that he feels.

God is love, and love enters into both the joys and pain of those that are loved. John wrote, "Whoever loves God must also love his brother". Our hearts should break with sorrow at the way our brother is treated. We should grieve at the sin that causes him grief. We should weep with him.

I don't understand, but I bear no ill-will to anybody.

Gordon Wilson

Gordon Wilson is the man whose daughter died when they were both buried in the rubble after the Enniskillen bombing in Northern Ireland. A writer, David Dale, says, "The world is infinitely richer because of the response of those who have allowed their suffering to take them to places unknown to those who have trodden the more untroubled way."

It is the way in which we respond to the wounds we receive that helps not only our own healing but also how other people view their troubles.

Because Gordon Wilson and his wife were able to accept what had happened, and knew God's grace upholding them, bitterness failed to take hold in their hearts. Not only must this have given a sense of freedom in their lives, but their attitude could only help others. What we are rubs off on those around us. Dissatisfaction and resentment at our problems can only incline people to our way of thinking, whilst the showing of love and forgiveness strengthens.

To be able to go without understanding the way that God is leading us is the meaning of faith. To do it without ill-will reveals God to other people.

Nay, whether God comes to his children with a rod or a crown, if he come himself with it, it is well.

Samuel Rutherford

Surely, the whole point of suffering is that if God is in it then all must be well. It is our God who is the centre of our life, not the circumstances that crowd in upon us. In a sense these must be secondary. For the Christian life is seeking to love and obey God. It also means accepting from his hand that which comes into it.

This may seem too simplistic, for if we could easily accept then suffering would not be suffering. Instead, the suffering has to be borne, but keeping our attention fixed on God means that we can draw from him the consolation and strength that we need.

Rutherford suggests that if it is only through suffering that we can get to know Jesus, then suffering is welcome. If bitterness must come before the joy, then the joy is worth it all. This can be understood as we allow God into our life and he becomes the one above all others in our love and desire. We may question but still trust, wrestle but still believe. Our God understands all of this, but our understanding must be of his love; his unswerving faithfulness; and the abundance of his grace.

The tree which responds vigorously to the wrenching winds and bending snow grows tough and strong and durable.

Philip Keller

When a tree withstands the blasts of the weather it grows up tall and strong. The more it withstands, the stronger it grows, and as it becomes strong, so the blasts are less able to move it.

Often those who have had to weather storms in their lives seem to have a quietness and strength about them that says more than words. As a tree stands firm, and is beautiful in its grandeur, so are they able to stand upright, in seemingly whatever is happening to them.

Psalm 1 speaks of the man whose "delight is in the law of the Lord . . . he is like a tree planted by streams of water". As the tree through its roots searches and draws up into itself the fresh water, so is the person who searches God's word and lives by it. Strong roots enable the tree to stand, just as to be rooted in God's word enables the Christian to be strong.

We sometimes think that we can weather the storms in our own strength and we try to do so. We may even turn away from God to prove our independence. Happy is the moment when we realize that we cannot.

When the flood of pain has passed over the soul, what remains alive can be considered genuine.

Carlo Carretto

It is perhaps as one goes further along the Christian path that one realizes the tapering of the way. It is almost as if everything has to be pushed back, and there comes a concentration, a singleness of purpose. Stranger still, it is as if one is being gentled along; through the situations that cause revaluation; into the darkness that causes joy only when the light is reached; through pain that makes us call out for the near presence of the one who can help.

We need to reach the understanding that we have to be freed from all that encumbers us and is not love. There needs to be purification; a total submission; the desire for holiness. God is continually seeking to help us to reach this understanding, for us to want to be like him. As the waves ride over us it is as if he watches to see what will be taken away — and what will remain.

At the same time we have to realize that God does not rejoice in our pain; he takes us through it himself and gives to us all the help that we are willing to accept.

Jesus remained faithful when his heart was breaking, when the cup was bitter and when his companions were weak.

Sinclair Ferguson

The crunch point for Jesus came after the Passover supper when he went with the disciples out to Gethsemane. He had already passed through two bitter experiences — facing the betrayal of Judas and Peter's avowal, and the knowledge that the disciples would abandon him.

In the garden he met with his Father, and it was here that he asked if the cup could be taken away. In the same breath he was confirming his desire to do the will of God; and the scene was set. It is in the will that decisions have to be taken, commitments made. Jesus may have been overcome for a moment, but there had never really been any doubt that he wanted only to do the will of his Father. He was ready to go through all that that meant.

There may come a time when we have to look at a situation as it is and reach a decision about commitment. We may have our own Gethsemane, where alone we face God. It is a place where we can show him our heart, but it is also the place where he wants us to give him our will and our trust.

We must be sincere in our sufferings as in everything else.

Thomas Merton

It is difficult to face up to ourselves when pain and weakness cause us to realize what they are making of us; when we are no longer as independent as we would wish; when so much more has to be given to others to do and we become aware of the ways in which they react.

Mistakenly, we may feel that those around are beginning to despise us, that we no longer have any worth in their eyes. We may have to learn to accept love without being able to give or do anything in return. These things have to be faced and as Merton suggests, we learn to suffer well.

When Paul said that we can do all things through Christ, he meant everything. With the awareness of Christ in us and in those around us, we can tackle the results of weakness, as in days gone by we may have tackled what seemed greater things.

Our worth as people does not diminish in God's eyes. We can show that he is with us in our suffering as we accept, not only the pain, but also all that it brings with it of dependence on others.

We may lose everything on earth, but we shall inherit everything in heaven.

John Stott

It was Jesus who said, ‘‘Blessed are those who are persecuted for righteousness’ sake, for theirs is the kingdom of heaven’’, and it is true that as Christians we should expect suffering in this world. Joined with Christ we take his values, and they are values to which, so often, the world does not subscribe.

There are still countries where men and women are persecuted for their faith. Where belonging to Christ and seeking to live the Christian life can mean imprisonment. Where persecution can mean loss of livelihood; where you can be despised; physically harmed; and property despoiled.

Although we may not be suffering in such extreme ways, yet as fellow believers we are one with them. Refusing to recognize this is paramount to Peter’s denial. We are ‘‘one of them’’, and the reason for any persecution that we may suffer in the daily round, is Christ himself. We should indeed ‘‘rejoice and be glad’’ to be counted alongside the One who has given us our life.

We may then, as disciples, have to suffer, but as John Stott reminds us, the other side of the coin is our inheritance.